Discovering your connected Self

Mohan Raskutti

A contemporary philosophical
exploration of the Brahma Sutras

Preface

Seeking answers to the perplexities of one's existence has been a pre-occupation of humankind since time immemorial. Abundant philosophical and metaphysical texts have originated over time from various corners of the globe in response to such seeking. Some, a very few, survive the test of time.

The Upanishads, Brahma Sutras and the Bhagavad Gita which constitute the Vedanta texts is one such body of knowledge that has not merely survived but forms, along with the Mahabharata, a vibrant living ethos of innumerable followers for generations.

Vedanta is the *anta* (end) or gist of the Vedas (Religious and philosophical texts originating from India). Vedanta deals with the *Jnana* or knowledge portion of the Vedas. The content of Vedanta texts is not mere speculation. It is the authentic record of actual transcendental experiences consisting of Self-realization achieved by *Rishis* or seers.

Vedas

The Vedas are the foundation of Hindu philosophy. The contents of the Vedas are revelations (*Srutis*) of *Atman* (spiritual principle of Self or *Brahman* in the individual) to the Rishis (ascetics, seers) in *Samadhi* (state of deep meditation). The revelations are impersonal, imperishable and ever-present. They are realizable by anyone in a state of Samadhi. The Vedas have taken shape over centuries of deep philosophical traditions dating back to 6000BCE and beyond.

It is essential to understand the terms *Samadhi* and 'revelations'. *Samadhi* is a state of being achieved through deep meditation wherein one is in in a state of pure awareness. It is a state of transcendence beyond one's physical and mental states.

In such a state of pure awareness and transcendence, one achieves realization of truths that lie beyond one's 'normal' existence in the world around us as we know it.

Such dimensions of awareness lead to one's inner core, one's *Atman* (spiritual principle of Self or Brahman in the individual) 'revealing' itself as truth (Sat).

Seven Rishis or seers (Saptarishis) are considered to be the first ones to achieve *Samadhi* (a state of being achieved through deep meditation wherein one is in in a state of pure awareness). They were the initial recipients of the revelations. These *Saptarishis* are referenced in the Jaiminya Upanishad Brahmana 2.218-226 and are considered to be the fountainheads of the Vedas. The *Saptarishis* are: Agasthya, Atri, Bhardwaja, Gautam, Jamadagni, Vashistha and Vishwamitra. The truths of these revelations are further validated and supported by the Brahma Sutras of Badrayana and the Bhagavad Gita of Shri Krishna. Veda Vyasa is the author of the Vedas.

Timeline of the Vedas

The Vedic timeline extends back to 6-8 millennia before the current era (BCE). Astronomical observations recorded in the Rig Veda pertain to those times. Extending back to 6000 BCE, the timeline of the Rig Veda extends through to 1500 BCE when the last hymns of the Rig Veda are estimated to have been completed. The Rig Veda is first of the four Vedas - the others being the Sama Veda, Yajur Veda and Atharva

Veda. The last of the Vedas – the Atharva Veda in its final oral form is estimated to have been completed around 900 BCE.

The rishis and sages of the land at that time decided that the Vedas should be placed in writing; if they were to be preserved. Various sages like Vasishtha, Agastya, Marichi, Atri, Angiras and Vishwamitra have hymns in written form attributed to them in the Rig Veda. Of the Atharva Veda, it is said that Veda Vyasa (of Mahabharat fame) and Maha Atharvan, collected and put this wisdom into writing.

Structure of the Vedas and the Upanishads

The Upanishads focus on the knowledge (*Jnana*) aspect of the Vedas and constitute its philosophical portion. They reveal the subtle and deep spiritual truths of the Vedas. The other (preceding) portions of each Veda are the hymns (Mantra-Samhitas), the explanations of Mantras or rituals (Brahmanas) and explanations of some of the esoteric rites and rituals (Aranyakas).

There are 108 Upanishads of which 13 are principal or *mukhya* Upanishads and the rest minor. The complete list of Upanishads is provided in the Muktitopanishad.

The principal (*mukhya*) Upanishads are Aitereya, Kaushitaki, Taittiriya, Katha, Shvetasvatara, Maitrayani, Brihadaranyaka, Isha, Kena, Chandogya, Mandukya, Mundaka and Prashna.

Alignment of the Vedas to the main Upanishads is as follows:

Aitereya and Kaushitaki Upanishads constitute the knowledge (*Jnana*) portion of the Rig Veda.

Similarly, Chandogya and Kena Upanishads align with Sama Veda;
Taittiriya, Katha, Svetasvatara and Maitrayani Upanishads align with Krishna Yajur Veda;

Brhadaranyaka and Isa Upanishads align with Shukla Yajur Veda; and

Mundaka, Mandukya and Prasna Upanishads align with Atharva Veda.

The other (non-*mukhya*) Upanishads associated with the Vedas are listed in Appendix 2.

Structure of the Brahma Sutras

Attributed to Badarayana, the Brahma Sutras is a foundational text that systematizes and summarizes Vedanta philosophy's spiritual principles as *Sutras* or aphorisms. It is estimated to have been completed in its surviving form between 450 BCE and 200 CE.

The aphorisms *(Sutras)* of the Brahma Sutras reconcile and summarize the statements of the numerous Upanishads. Thereby making the Brahma Sutras a repository of the fundamental philosophical concepts and principles of the Vedas.

Sutras are concise aphorisms. They provide the condensed essence of each topic or main heading *(Adhikaranam)*. This allows for deep reflection and realization of the concepts in each *Adhikaranam*.

Reiteration and repetition are striking features of the Brahma Sutras. This is so as to enable focused study *(Abhyasa)***, reflection and realization of the principles and philosophy outlined in it.**

The Brahma Sutras is structured into four chapters. Each chapter in turn is broken down into four sections or *Padas*. Each section covers a number of main headings or topics *(Adhikaranams)*. Each *Adhikaranam* is constituted of a number of aphorisms *(Sutras)*.

The 555 *Sutras* of the Brahma Sutras are structured into 191 *Adhikaranams*.

The complete list of Chapters *(Adhyayas)*, *Adhikaranams* (Topics) and *Sutras* (Aphorisms)is provided in Appendix 1.

The first chapter *(Samanvaya adhyaya)* defines the unified concept of *Brahman*. The second *(Avirodha adhyaya)* counters the refutations of other opposing philosophies to establish uniformity in understanding of the concept of *Brahman* as laid down in chapter 1. The third *(Sadhana adhyaya)* deals with practice *(Sadhana)* to attain *Brahman* and the fourth *(Phala adhyaya)* focuses on the fruits of Self-realization.

Author's Note

This text (Reflection series part 1) is based on Chapter 1 of the Brahma Sutras. Separate individual texts forming Reflection series parts 2 to 4 will follow; corresponding to chapters 2 to 4 of the Brahma Sutras.

The first chapter of the Brahma Sutras (titled *Samanvayadhyaya* - which is structured from the two Sanskrit words *Samanvay* meaning connected sequence and *adhyaya* meaning chapter) closely examines the reality of existence in general and the human condition in particular. The philosophical examination focuses on the fundamental human attributes of one's sense of self in the context of manifested reality. Such an examination leads to providing a set of principles that assist in understanding, defining and clarifying one's sense of self in the manifested experientiality we find ourselves in.

The aspiration of this English interpretation of the first chapter of the Brahma Sutras is to share the philosophical heights that I experienced as I read, thought about and discovered in the profound depths of wisdom that lie within each aphorism *(Sutra)*, each main heading *(Adhikaranam)*, each section *(pada)* in the first chapter *(Samanvaya adhyaya)*. I am by no stretch of imagination a Vedic scholar, whatever its connotations. I am merely an explorer of the reality of human existence.

All interpretations of the contents of the Brahma Sutras (and other related Vedanta texts) are my own and based on my current state of understanding. I am discovering a treasure trove, which I want to share in the form of this text.

Structure of this text

Each of the eight sections in this text aligns with a number of main topics or headings *(Adhikaranams)* of Chapter 1 of the Brahma Sutras. Appendix 1 provides the list and a brief description of each *Adhikaranam* in chapter 1.

Section 1 in this text outlines the human condition and the circumstances that the reader (as a manifested being in Nature) finds themself in - as a perplexed yearner seeking answers to their existence in Nature. It also highlights the attributes of such a yearner that qualifies them to seek out what may lie beyond their current state of manifested being.

Section 2 provides a response to the yearner by focusing on Nature's essence of transience and plurality. It follows this on by suggesting that a satisfactory response can only be what Nature is 'not' i.e. non-transient and non-plural. The concept of Self or *Brahman* is introduced as a wholesome response.

Section 3 follows on from section 2 in pointing out that the principle of *Brahman* lies beyond what the yearner can comprehend because of the yearner's current state as a manifested being in Nature and beholden to what means and tools (like the senses, mind and intellect) Nature offers. The only way to transcend the limitations, this section suggests, is deep reflection and meditation aided by the Vedantic texts (Brahma Sutras, Upanishads and the Bhagavad Gita).

Section 4 points out that the consistent focus of Vedantic texts is the Self (*Brahman*). The reader of these texts has to bear this in mind at all times when studying and interpreting these texts.

Section 5 reasons that continuity in Nature's transience and plurality is provided by the anchored presence of *Brahman* or Self as non-transient, sentient singularity.

Section 6 discusses the pervasiveness of the non-transient, sentient singularity of Self (*Brahman*) in all manifested beings in Nature; indeed in Nature itself. It also introduces the concept of *Manomaya* (The power of the mind – Mano - by which the universe becomes manifest; the illusion or appearance of the phenomenal world) as that aspect of Self (*Brahman*) that anchors the manifested being's mind, thoughts and actions of each being to manifest all that exists in Nature.

Section 7 elaborates on the Self (*Brahman*) as non-transient, sentient singularity that pervades Nature and what lies beyond Nature itself; thereby qualifying as being its source or origin.

Having started from the human condition of the yearner in section 1 and developing a response to the yearning, the first seven sections detail some of the key concepts or principles of the Brahma Sutras. Section 8 wraps up this text by providing a potential pathway for the yearner from the discovery of the concepts through to reflection, realization and eventual transcendence to the Self or *Brahman*.

Numerous quotes from various Vedanta texts (Upanishads and Brahma Sutras) are referred to throughout this text. Each quote is attributed to the specific source next to each quote. Each quote itself is not a literal translation from Sanskrit to English. It is modified and interpreted by the author without losing the essence or intent of the original Sanskrit quote. Sanskrit words are italicized throughout this text. Numbered reference to various texts (as listed in in the 'Reference section) are provided as appropriate.

Terminology used in this text

Manifested being (*Jiva*) – Any entity in Nature that demonstrates attributes of transience, plurality and insentience as follows:

> ➤ Transience in time – That which is constantly changing in time. Starting from its origin through growth, plateau, decline and eventual demise in Nature.
>
> ➤ Plurality in space – That which is distinguishable in Nature by attributes of shape, size, colour etc. i.e. that which conforms to Nature's essence of plurality in space.

9

➢ Insentience in that it conforms to Nature's physical and spiritual laws like the laws of cause and effect (*Karma*).

Examples of such manifested beings include human beings, flora, fauna, mountains and oceans.

Self or **Universal Self (*Brahman*)** – is the principle of non-transience in time, non-plurality (singularity) in space and sentience as follows:

➢ Perennial, without conforming to Nature's law of transience in time i.e. without having origin, growth, plateau, decline and eventual demise.

➢ Non-plurality or Singularity which is that which is not subject to Nature's attributes of shape, size, colour etc. i.e. that which does not conform to Nature's essence of plurality in space).

➢ Sentient (i.e. aware of and not subject to Nature's laws of cause and effect, action and reaction).

Self is the antithesis of a manifested being. Self is awareness that is untouched and unbeholden to laws of any ilk e.g. laws of Nature.

Individual Self (*Atman* or *Atma*) – The quantum of the Self (*Brahman*) that permeates and co-exists with each manifested being in Nature.

Nature– Phenomenal dimension of time and space where transience and plurality play out.

Sat (truth) – Essence of the Self (*Brahman*); being the pure non-transient, singular sentience.

Pradhana (prime, main, prime) – Prime or chief cause or creative principle of Nature.

Acknowledgements

This text is a result of the author reading, listening to and studying various philosophical books, papers and talks (both in hard copy and digital forms). All these works are freely available in the public domain. The main sources are listed in the section titled 'Reference'.

Specifically, the author would like to acknowledge the philosophy detailed in the following text which was used as the basis for the author's study:

> "Brahma Sutras - Text, word-to-word meaning, translation and commentary by Sri Swami Sivananda" (Published by The Divine Life Society, P.O. P.O. Shivanandanagar – 249 192, Tehri-Garhwal, Uttarakhand, Himalayas, India – 2008).

Valuable insights and feedback provided by my wife Bhavani has been vital in bringing this text to life. With her meaningful questions and deep insights, she has been instrumental in sharpening my thoughts and adding significantly to the readability of this text. Not to mention her ideas on formatting this text; based on her experience as a published author herself.

A number of discussions, heated at times, that I have had with close friends has been invaluable in shaping this text.

Last but not least, various commentaries and interpretations provided in significant writings of the Brahma Sutras and Upanishads in the public domain (as referenced in this text) has provided numerous 'eureka' moments in my personal spiritual growth, which indeed flows into this text.

Contents

1. Discovering restlessness and yearning

> "I didn't know then what I wanted, but the ache for it was palpable."
> — Sue Monk Kidd, The Mermaid Chair

There resides in each one of us a restlessness (*vibhrama*) in varying degrees that drives one to learn, grow and achieve one's potential in any of several activities or professions. Be it as an artist, businessperson, sportsperson, social worker, politician, homemaker, scientist.... The list goes on.

Restlessness acts as a motivation to achieve varying degrees of satisfaction and fulfillment in any chosen sphere of activity. Fulfillment is invariably followed by emptiness, a vacuum. Which leads to further restlessness to fill in the vacuum. Ad infinitum.

Restlessness can be attributed to one's existence in cyclical transience (*asarata*) and plurality (*anaikya*) - imperatives when dwelling in Nature. It is an existence that, out of necessity, enables one to develop skills and habits as conditioned responses for survival in Nature's playground of transience and plurality. Cyclical transience and plurality are the very essence of Nature.

Some amongst us recognize and sense the increased awareness of the continuing cycles of restlessness followed by effort then fulfillment ad infinitum.

1.1 Restlessness and yearning

Once recognized within oneself, restlessness can lead to a yearning (*vena*) within us to explore what may lie beyond the cycles of restlessness and fulfillment. Indeed what may lie beyond the essential cyclicality, the perennial transience of one's existence in the experiential world; an existence where it seems that change is the only constant in life!

Following are a few recognizable signs of one's yearning, if and when it arises:

> An 'awareness' of a widening chasm between one's 'individual Self' (the one within that is aware of the restlessness) and the repetitive impermanence of the experiential world. It is an awareness that is normally gained after exploring, witnessing and experiencing life to varying degrees

> Awareness of a deep sense of diminished enjoyment of and detachment from the living body's actions and resultant fruits of such actions

> An increasing sense of déjà vu, a predictability, in what is seen, heard, witnessed and participated in as part of one's existence in Nature

1.2 Yearning and readiness

The first aphorism (sutra) in the Brahma Sutras sums up the yearning and readiness to explore beyond transience and plurality thus: 'Athato Brahmajijnasa' translating to 'Now, then, afterwards (i.e. as an immediate consequence of one's current state - now and for all time to come), a desire for the knowledge of the Self (Brahman) arises'. Thereby highlighting that enquiry into the restlessness (and yearning for an appropriate response) is a result of achieving a state of readiness for embarking on the quest for what may lie beyond one's immersion in cyclical transience. The readiness itself not being transient i.e. not just present fleetingly and dissipating over time but persisting beyond now for all time.

When the 'awareness' of the yearning arises and persists now, then, afterwards (i.e. for all time), that is when readiness to explore the essence of one's existence and what may lie beyond is signaled.

Over and above the rising and persistence of the awareness, readiness is fortified by acquisition of four-fold preliminary qualifications as follows :

> *Nityaanitya-vastuviveka* i.e. discrimination *(Vastuviveka)* between the eternal *(Nitya)* and the non-eternal *(Aanitya)*; thereby seeking out, acceptance and fondness of that which is not transient but lasting and real

> *Ihamutraphalabhogavairaa* i.e. Proper perspective on the enjoyment in this life and what may lie beyond *(Ihamutra)*, and growing detachment from actions *(Vairaga)* and the fruits thereof *(Phalabhoga)*.

> Possession of virtues (as follows) that help in controlling that which constitutes one's manifested being:

   • Control of the mind *(Sama)*
   • Control of the outward looking senses *(Dama)*
   • Non-obsessiveness with worldly enjoyments and decreased dependence on and preoccupation with sensory objects i.e. objects that appeal to the sense of taste, touch, sight, smell and sound
   • Endurance of discomfort and pain *(Titiksha)*
   • Faith in one's ways to address one's yearning e.g. meditating on the contents of the Brahma Sutras, Upanishads *(Sraddha)* and relentlessly endeavouring towards realization of and transcendence to being united with one's individual Self and indeed the universal Self
   • Deep focus and concentration on putting things together with the right perspective *(Samadhana)*.

This provides the gateway to meditation and
transcendence from the realm of Nature with its
constraints of time and space

➢ Desire for liberation (*Mumukshutva*).

Yearning based on the attributes above, when given
into, leads to discovering, reflecting on, realizing one's
individual Self and transcending to be one with the
universal Self.

Readiness can be summarized as one's ability to
gradually grow out of and detach oneself from the
mundane and reach out to a state beyond the
experiential – a state of being beyond Nature –
dwelling in the reality of awareness. Such awareness
can lead to attainment of freedom and a state of
calmness, a state of bliss and freedom. These are
attributes that enable one to navigate through one's
existence in Nature (with its transience and plurality)
while anchored on the reality of awareness that is the
sentient Self.

2. The experiential world and reality beyond

"Where there is plurality, as it were, there one
sees another. But when Self only is all there is,
then how should one see another?"
(Brihadaranyaka Upanishad III-7-22)

Born out of the yearning to explore what may lie
beyond one's existence in Nature and what may lie
beyond Nature itself comes the need to understand
Nature.

The experiential world of Nature is governed by
laws that are based on time and space, transience and
plurality. Nature's essence is transience in time and
plurality (multiplicity) in space.

**The reality beyond Nature's transience and
plurality that is yearned for can only be what Nature
is not!**

To be 'other than' one's experiential world in Nature,
implies being:

➢ Beyond transience and time i.e. being unconstrained by
   transient concepts of origins and demises i.e. being ever-
   lasting, immortal, imperishable.

➢ Beyond plurality and differentiation i.e. being beyond our
   experiential world in Nature that is based on objects that
   are characterized and differentiated based on Nature's
   attributes of time, space and their constraints viz.
   differentiated identities based on size, colour, shape, age
   etc.

➢ Beyond insentience. Nature's manifestations essentially
   have to be in conformance with Nature's laws of
   transience and plurality. Being unlike and beyond such
   conformance implies being above and beyond the

insentience of conformance. Insentience is blind following and conformance to Nature's laws of transience and plurality. It is objectified behaviour e.g. behaviour like any rock that conforms to the laws of gravity; and beings driven to conform to Nature's laws of cause and effect *(Karma)*. Sentient awareness on the other hand, enables experiencing plurality and transience in Nature without necessarily being part of it.

➢ Beyond *Karma* (action and reaction). Action and reaction, cause and effect require a medium (time and space) to play out in; along with a differentiation between individual objects i.e. plurality. Time and space are in the realm of Nature and its laws. Resting beyond such actions and the fruits of such actions and reactions is a state of being in a reality beyond Karma.

➢ Beyond movement in space and time - movement implies change in both time and space.

➢ Beyond manifestation – i.e. not manifested like all beings and objects in Nature.

The reality that so offers complete and unfettered freedom from transience, plurality and insentience is Self *(Brahman)*.

Being non-transient, non-plural and sentient, Self is one single whole. It is non-changing, non-plural, sentient awareness with none of Nature's attributes of time and space. With unconstrained awareness, it experiences and perceives all that is for what it is and what it can be. It is a state of being beyond Nature, beyond time, space, beyond insentient manifestation, beyond *Karma* (action and reaction).

2.1 Self *(Brahman)*

Self exists by itself in complete and unfettered freedom from transience and interdependence i.e.

unconstrained by time and space. Awareness that is Self provides a platform to perceive and experience Nature for what it is – transient and non-real. Something to be witnessed and experienced with a sense of detached enjoyment, i.e. not partaking in Nature's play of action and reaction – *Karma*.

Passive yet fully aware witnessing and experiencing the transience and plurality in Nature is one dimension of the power of awareness of the sentient Self. Actively exercising choice in interpreting and indeed impacting on and shaping (through the agents of the Self viz. tools like arms and legs, senses like eyes and ears, thinking mind etc. that manifested beings are endowed with) Nature (within its insentient laws) is another dimension of the power of Self *(Brahman)*.

When so actively exercised, the power of awareness of sentient Self does indeed become the cause of outcomes in Nature's play of action and reaction. Accumulating every outcome in Nature born out of such individual causes and extrapolating ad infinitum, it becomes plausible to surmise that the awareness of sentient Self, a universally Aware Self, is the cause for all that plays out in Nature!

So it is surmised in the second *Sutra* as *'Janmadi Asya Yatah'* - The origin or source of the 'Here and Now' in the manifested universe (as it exists at any point in time in any point in space) is the Self *(Brahman)* witnessing, experiencing and indeed causing all that is in Nature.

Further quotes from the Upanishads relating to this topic is in Appendix 3.

3. Discovering Self (Brahman)

"In that quality of attention there is silence, unfathomable silence. That silence has never been touched by thought, and only then that for which man has searched from time immemorial, something sacred, something nameless, supreme, comes" – Krishnamurti, Mind Without Measure

An object exists independent of anyone wanting to understand it. Understanding an object is dependent on the abilities and capabilities of the one trying to understand viz. the perceiver. The Self (Brahman) is no exception.

Normal human abilities to perceive and understand are aided by the senses, mind and intellect. These have inherent ranges and limitations. Additionally, individual perceptions and understanding are colored by the makeup of the individual being. One's inherent genetic makeup, social environment, upbringing etc. color the perception of the same objects or events. Consequently leading to different interpretations of the same phenomenon or object by different viewers and interpreters.

The knowledge of the real nature of a thing does not depend on the notions of man but only on the thing itself. The knowledge of the Self (Brahman) also depends altogether on the thing, i.e., Brahman itself. Knowledge is not an effect of volition while action depends entirely on will. Knowledge depends on the object perceived. Discovery, reflection on, realization of and transcendence to Brahman is object-based knowledge (Vastu Tantra); i.e. it depends on the reality of the object. It is not knowledge based on volition

(*Purusha Tantra*); i.e. it does not depend on volition. It is not something to be accomplished by action. *Brahman* is not an object of the senses. It has no connection with other means of knowledge. The senses are finite and dependent. They have only external things for their objects, not *Brahman* nor *Atman* - one's internal Self. The senses are in their essence so constituted that they focus on external objects.

Knowledge of Brahman cannot come through mere reasoning. You can attain this knowledge through intuition or revelation. Intuition is the final result of the enquiry into *Brahman*. The object of enquiry is an existing substance. You will have to know this only through direct intuition or cognition (*Aparakosha-anubhuti*) or experience (*Anubhava*). Hearing the revelations (*Srutis*), reflecting on what has been heard (*Manana*), profound meditation (*Nididhyasana*) on *Brahman* leads to intuition. The state of mind that involves thought of *Brahman* alone (*Brahmakara Vritti*) is reached through deep meditation. It is the final state of the mind before it becomes one with the absolute truth, at which point there is no mind at all and the Self is in eternal liberation. It is generated from one's Self in complete awareness (*Sattvic Antahkarana* – true internal awareness). It is aided by the instructions of a *Guru* (spiritual teacher), who has understood the real significance of '*Tat Tvam Asi*' (that thou art). This *Brahmakara Vritti* (thought of *Brahman* alone) destroys the primitive ignorance (*Mula-Avidya*), the root cause of all bondage. When the ignorance or veil is removed in ordinary perception of objects, the mind assumes the form of the object. The mind sees through the veil (*Avarana-bhanga*) that envelops the object and sentient awareness (*Vritti-sahita-chaitanya*) reveals the object. Then only can one cognize the object.

As *Brahman* is beyond the reach of the senses and the intellect, such awareness of the Self can be apprehended only on the authority of the *Srutis* which are infallible and contain the spiritual experiences of realized seers or sages. The scriptures illumine all things like a searchlight. Scriptures provide a comprehensive understanding of the Self (*Brahman*). *Srutis* furnish information about what is not known from other sources. Lack of understanding of the *Srutis* leads to inability to know and experience that pure 'awareness that is Self' –*Brahman*.

Awareness that is Self (*Brahman*) cannot be achieved by other means of knowledge independent of the *Srutis*. *Brahman* being non-manifested (i.e. formless, colorless, attribute less) cannot be grasped by the senses nor by direct perception. Any other sources of knowledge can supplement one's understanding and experiencing the aware Self (*Brahman*) but only after a true understanding is established by the *Srutis*.

The *Vedantic* school (which is based on the Vedanta philosophy as professed in the Upanishads, Brahma Sutras and Bhagavad Gita) maintains that the awareness that is one's individual Self is identical with the awareness that is the universal Self. Awareness that is Self (*Brahman*) destroys *Avidya* or ignorance which is the root of all misinterpretations and is the seed of this *Samsara* (Nature's transience and plurality leading to cycles of origin, growth, plateau, decay and demise to which every manifestation in the material world is bound) or worldly life. The yearning for and single-minded focus on awareness that is *Brahman* (Self) alone destroys *Avidya* or ignorance; leading to the attainment of Self. Hence an enquiry about 'Self' (Brahman) through the study of the *Srutis* whose focus is Self (Brahman) alone is worthwhile and should be undertaken.

In summary, discovering, reflecting on, realizing and transcending to pure awareness that is 'Self' (Brahman), demand capabilities beyond sensory perceptions and intellectual reasoning. They need the *Srutis* and any other knowledge aligned to that which is contained in and conveyed by the *Srutis*.

3.1 Awareness that is Self (Brahman)

Developing skills to enable deep reflection leading on to realization, often needs an experienced teacher who understands the concept of awareness that is Self, and can provide the skills and tools to enable one to take steps towards realizing it. Tools include texts like the Brahma Sutras that summarize and outline the philosophical ideas and principles of the reality of *Brahman*; as contained in the *Srutis*.

It is worth reiterating the origin of the Vedas, Upanishads and Brahma Sutras here. The Vedas are *Srutis* (revelations) of the Self (Brahman) or *Atman* (individual Self) to the *Rishis* (seers, ascetics) in *Samadhi* (state of deep meditation). The revelations are impersonal, imperishable and ever-present. They are realizable by anyone in a state of *Samadhi*. *Samadhi* is a state of deep meditation wherein one achieves and indeed becomes one with a state of pure awareness that is Self. It is a state of transcendence beyond one's physical and mental states. In such a state of pure awareness and transcendence, one achieves oneness with dimensions of truths that lie beyond that in one's 'normal' existence in the world around us as we know it. Such dimensions of awareness lead to one's inner core, one's *Atman* or *Brahman*, one's 'individual Self' 'revealing' itself as Truth.

The third aphorism *(sutra)* in the Brahms sutras states–'*Sastra Yonitvat (knowledge of the Srutis contained in the scriptures i.e. Vedantic texts – Upanishads, Brahma Sutras and Bhagavad Gita – along with the Mahabharata are the source or means of right knowledge of Brahman)'*.

Learning to embrace the knowledge and skills as above also requires shedding some skills that one has acquired and practiced over time. Skills to be foregone include being wedded to transient material attachments, perceiving, seeking and promoting differences rather than connectivity, commonality and unity.

The enquiry of *Brahman* does not depend on the performance of any acts. Attainment of 'awareness that is Self' is achievable through deep reflection or meditation on *Brahman* and the truths declared by Vedantic texts and not through mere reasoning. Pure reason *(Suddha Buddhi)* is a help in Self-realization. It investigates and reveals the truths of the Scriptures. It also has a place in the means of Self-realization. But perverted intellect *(Viparita Buddhi)* is a great hindrance. It keeps one far away from the truth.

Individual attributes of readiness (as outlined earlier) go a long way in enabling the acquisition of required skills.

Material attachment (including attachment to one's own body, emotions like fear etc.) is considered the root cause of ignorance *(Avidya)*– bondage to impermanence.

When the veil of ignorance is removed, one directly experiences connection to, oneness with and complete absorption in the singular awareness that is 'Self'. Discovering, reflecting on, realizing and transcending to such awareness that is Self is the prerogative of every being in Nature. Readiness to do so, however, depends entirely on one's ability to gradually grow out of and detach oneself from the mundane and reach out to a state beyond the experiential. Readiness is "Devotion to *Brahman*, firm in intent, seeking oneness with *Brahman*, carrying the fuel of yearning within one's individual Self *(Brahman)*."(Prasna Upanishad I-1).

4.   Brahma Sutras and Self
(Brahman)

"This world was but one real truth (Sat) of the
'Self' in the beginning. In it, all that exists has its
own individual Self. It is true. It is the 'Self'"
(Chhandogya Upanishad chapter VI).

The reality of Self is a consistent reality within which
Nature's transience is played out in all its glory. It
offers a platform for every being in Nature to witness
and experience transience - cycles of creation,
preservation and dissolution in Nature.

Discovering, reflecting on and realization of an
awareness that is one's individual Self is the first step in
ascending to transcendence to the universal Self -
beyond transience, plurality and insentience.

The process of discovery starts with acceptance of
the reality of one's immersion in transience, plurality
and insentience – a natural state of existence for one
immersed in Nature with an avowed acceptance of all
things in Nature; from one's origin, growth, plateau,
decline and demise. Such acceptance awakens the
awareness that is Self within oneself (the one that is
aware of the restlessness). It is an awareness that
witnesses but is not part of Nature's grand stage; an
awareness that is in essence independent of rather than
attached to and immersed like one's manifested being.
It is that part of oneself which is different from and
independent from all other components of one's
manifestation viz. one's body, senses, mind and
intellect. Such acceptance of one's immersion in
Nature's transience, plurality and insentience leads to

the discovery of the so far unexplored individual Self. This is followed by an increasing attachment to and awareness that is one's individual Self. Awareness that is the Self leads to a deep sense of independence that provides a different perspective of one's experiences in Nature.

The secret of empowering oneself to be one with Self lies in understanding that it requires no action to be so. It is not a result of one's willing or doing. It is a consequence of understanding it for what it is and reflecting on it thereby shedding the veil of ignorance (*Avidya*) that prevents one from realizing it; whence one is drawn into it.

Awareness that is Self, when realized is what one's Self really is – non-transient, singular, sentience - *Tat tvam asi* (That thou art). It is a state of bliss without fear, a state of emancipation, enlightenment, liberation and release (*Moksha*). The awareness that is 'Self (*Brahman*)' as the single universal principle is explicit and implicitly expressed in Vedanta texts; as highlighted by the following quote:

"In the beginning all this was *Brahman* (Self) only" (Aitereya Upanishad II-4-I-1);

The consistent focus in all Vedantic texts is on *Brahman* alone as the means to enlightened awareness that is Self, that which one already is (*Tat Twam Asi* - (Chhandogya Upanishad VI-8-7). Such singular consistent focus is what enables the Vedantic texts to provide the basis to enable realization of *Brahman*.

"This world was but one real truth (*Sat*) of the 'Self' in the beginning. In it, all that exists has its own individual awareness that is Self. It is true. It is the 'Self'" (Chhandogya Upanishad chapter VI).

4.1 Discovering consistency

Living with transience while anchoring oneself in Self requires associating with Self incessantly. This enables one to transcend the 'noise' of transience to the realm of Self while still having one's foot (in a manner of speaking) in the transience of Nature.

Association and oneness with Self calls for training oneself with unwavering focus on one's anchor – one's individual Self. This is necessary in order to enable detachment from transience and allow gradual transcendence into the realm of Self.

Reflecting on *"Tat Tvam Asi"* (That thou art i.e. the being within oneself - one's individual Self) provides the unwavering focus on awareness that is Self.

4.2 Oneness with Self

Transcendence is when one identifies with Self and its uniqueness. Once attained, everything else is known. Anchored in the one reality of Self (Brahman), one is free to witness Nature in all its transient glory - a transience and plurality that provides a world of countless names and forms.

Awareness that is Self enables understanding the inherent essence of transience and plurality of all objects in Nature. Oneness with Self is when one attains a state of realization that 'Self' (non-transient, singular sentience) is the only platform from which to witness and enjoy the transience, the cycles of creation, preservation and dissolution in Nature.

Highlighting the pervasiveness of the singular Self (Brahman), the *Srutis* declare the 'Self' to be the source: "All this springs from the Self" (Chhandogya Upanishad VII-2-6).

The term 'Self' here denotes a non-transient, singular, sentient aware being. The all-knowing *Brahman* is to be taken as the source of the world as per the uniform view of the Vedanta texts.

5. Individual Self (*Atman*)

"As rivers, flowing down, become indistinguishable on reaching the sea by giving up their names and forms, so also the illumined Self, having become freed from name and form, reaches the self-effulgent ocean that is the supreme Self" – Mundaka Upanishad

Every manifested being in Nature is bound by space and time. Riding the waves of time and space, each being is driven by its intrinsic attributes to successfully navigate the ups and downs of the transience and plurality in Nature. Attributes define what each being uniquely is (e.g. human, animal, male or female, winged or wingless etc.). Such beings can act in Nature's playground based on what it is endowed with (e.g. limbs or fins, lungs or gills etc.). Each manifested being adds to the multitudinous plurality of attributes of shape, size, color, form etc. in its limited existence in Nature's cycle of origin, growth, plateau, decline and demise. In such an existence, every manifested being is nevertheless connected to and sharing with other beings the one Self (*Brahman*).

Inscrutable to such beings is its own reality, the anchor, its individual Self within. Discovering such inscrutability is the start of one's transcendence born out of one's yearning. Further, aware acceptance of the reality of Self or *Brahman* is one's first step in discovering, reflecting on, realizing and eventually transcending to universal Self and its non-transient singular sentient reality.

The individual Self coexists with one's manifested being in Nature; each in their purest forms. Self is that whose essence is *Sat* (truth), which is unconstrained (by space, time, action and reaction), detached, blissful, an enjoyer of all that transpires in Nature's maelstrom of transience and plurality. The manifested being is the one that is constrained by laws of Nature within the realm of space and time, plurality and transience.

Both play essential roles to enable the being to navigate Nature's wonderland of color, shapes, forms and moods. The manifested being – body, senses and mind as its instruments navigates itself in Nature. The other, individual Self (*Brahman*), being an untouched, non-immersed charioteer as it were, enjoying the embodied being's ride in Nature with its manifested, transient brilliance, provides an anchor of non-transient, singular awareness to the manifested being.

"That which exists and dwells in every being and that which the individual embodied being, the manifested being does not know, that is the *Brahman* within" (Brihadaranyaka Upanishad III-7-3).

The subtlety of Self is described as the difference between "shade (the transience in the manifested being) and light (*Brahman*)" (Kathopanishad I-3-1).

5.1 Differentiation

Differentiating between the essence of Self within (one's individual Self) and the impermanent transient plurality of the manifested being is the key to discovering, reflecting, realizing and transcending to being one with the universal Self (*Brahman*).

Transience and plurality have its beginnings and endings, origins and demises. Self with its sentient non-transience and non-plurality resides in each being, distinguished from the insentient transience and plurality in Nature. Self is one's anchor, one's individual Self (*Tat Tvam Asi*).

"Know Self to be the charioteer, the body to be the chariot."(Kathopunishad I-3-3).

Here Self is represented as a charioteer anchoring the manifested being through its trans-migratory existence to final emancipation from transience and cyclicality (origin through growth, plateau, decline and eventual demise) in Nature.

5.2 Inscrutability of individual Self

The wonder in Nature is its seemingly limitless possibilities and probabilities of states to manifest itself in for each being in space and time. The manifestation that eventualizes being but one of innumerable possible and probable manifestations. Once manifested, each individual manifestation is governed by Nature's laws of action and reaction (*Karma*) in Nature's attributes of space and time.

Within such endless possibilities and probabilities, there is room for non-transience, non-plurality, non-manifestation - a reality of the oneness and singularity of Self. A state of being unbounded by and beyond time, space and the laws of Nature as one knows it. Discovering such frontiers is the realm of one who yearns; one who dwells in Self. "*Yo vijnane tishthan* (One who dwells in Knowledge)"(Brihadaranyaka Upanishad III-7-22).

Individual Self then becomes the realizable reality for such beings who yearn, immersed as those beings are in the Self. The difference between the plurality experienced by a manifested being and the individual Self within is one of limitation (*Upadhi*). The difference is merely the product of accepting and living within such limitations of its embodiment.

A pre-condition for a being in Nature, its raison d'etre is the limiting adjunct. It consists of the organs of sense and action in Nature and its transient plurality. Just as we make a distinction between the contents within the confines of a jar that in turn is immersed in a larger space pervaded by the universal content. "Where there is plurality, as it were, there one sees another. But when Self only is all there is, then how should one see another?" (Brihadaranyaka Upanishad III-7-22). Realizing the truth (*Sat*) of the non-reality of the self-imposed limitations (*Upadhi*) is when, it is argued, the world of plurality and transience dissolves in the sphere of true realization of Self (*Brahman*)!

"*Brahman* is the immortal, unseen seer, unheard hearer". There is no other seer but Self, there is no other thinker but Self, there is no other Knower but Self. This is the *Brahman*, the Ruler within, the Immortal. Everything else is unreal" (Brihadaranyaka Upanishad III-7-23).

5.3 Discovering connectedness

All manifested beings in Nature have their roots in the physicality of Nature and dissolve back into Nature's physicality. Be it into the soil, water or ether. "All manifested beings take their origin from the ether (*Akasa*), and return into the ether. Ether is greater than the beings, ether is their ultimate resort" (Chhandogya Upanishad I-9).

One's physicality, having its origins and eventual demise into Nature, is consequently transient and immersed in the plurality of Nature. One's individual

Self that is embedded within each embodied being, witnesses, perceives, experiences and enjoys the universe of transience in which it finds itself; enjoying Nature in full recognition of what it is – non-persistent and consequently unreal.

The essence of Self is the reality of non-transient, singular sentient awareness that offers complete and unfettered freedom from transience, insentience and plurality. Self is one single complete whole with none of Nature's attributes; all pervasive, non-manifested, boundless and everlasting; with unconstrained sentience i.e. awareness of all that is and what can be. It is an awareness to understand all that is within and beyond space and time.

6. Manomaya

"He who consists of the mind, whose body is
Prana (breath - the subtle body), whose
manifested form is transient in Nature, whose
resolve is true, enjoys in blissful detachment
from all actions triggered by expectations. This
enjoyer is *Brahman*" (Chhandogya Upanishad
III-14-2)

That which is awareness in the manifested being is
the individual Self *(Brahman)*. It is distinct from the
manifested being that consists of body, senses, mind
and intellect. It is that which, from a platform of non-
transience and non-plurality (oneness):

➢ Is aware of the faculties of the manifested being, i.e.
body, senses, mind and intellect

➢ Anchors the mind *(Mano)* and intellect to enable it to
discriminate between the eternal and the non-eternal
(Nitya-anitya-vastuviveka) i.e. enables the mind to:

   • Control itself *(Sama)*
   • Control the external senses *(Dama)*
   • Be non-obsessive with worldly enjoyments i.e. be
     non-compulsive in thinking of objects of senses
     (Uparati)
   • Endure pleasure and pain, heat and cold *(Titiksha)*
   • Rest in the non-transient, non-plural Self
     (Sraddha) and
   • So resting, have deep concentration *(Samadhana)*

➢ Provides the manifested being a proper perspective on
the enjoyment in this life and of the fruits of its actions
(Iham utrartha phala bhoga viraga)

➢ Projects through one's own mind all that is perceived in
Nature (with its transience and plurality). This gives rise to
the play of Karma, action and reaction in Nature; enabled

by the tools of action like the mind that triggers actions that are performed by the appendages for action e.g. the arms and legs and monitored by the senses.

6.1 Expectations

Expectations harbored by the mind drive actions in the anticipation of a specific set of outcomes. The expectation framework that each individual being has, is one's view of the world, of Nature and its workings. This is *Manomaya* (The power of the mind – Mano - by which the universe becomes manifest; the illusion or appearance of the phenomenal world).

Expectations based on a 'true' understanding of reality by the mind leads to fructification of expectations Conversely, unreal (untrue) understanding based on unawareness or limited awareness of Nature's laws of cause and effect leads to unfulfilled expectations.

The driver of actions is expectations. Without the driver, without expectations, there can be no action and no outcomes.

Cause and effect are inherent in Nature. Every cause produces an effect according to the laws of Nature. It is the interactions between cause and effect, action and reaction that are manifested in Nature. Nature provides for free play between actions and reactions. Players in Nature's stage can act at will to enjoy (or suffer) the consequential manifested outcomes. While the will to be and act is inherent in every being in Nature, the outcomes are no act of will. It is subject to Nature's vagaries (born out of the innumerable beings that exist and interact in Nature's plurality and transience) based on laws that govern cause and effect in Nature.

A manifested being in Nature is the outcome of its expectations and subsequent actions. The being becomes that what it now expects and resolves to be.

6.2 Discovering expectations

The tightrope of expectations in every manifested being dreams up all that subsequently transpires to its manifested being. This is followed up by actions in the grand interplay of multitudinous beings in Nature. While itself being non-embodied and consequently unable to act, individual Self (*Brahman*) within every manifested being enjoys the plurality and transience that comes out of the mind, its expectations, actions and outcomes. While itself being detached and uninvolved, the individual Self is an enjoyer in blissful detachment.

"He who consists of the mind, whose body is *Prana* (breath - the subtle body), whose manifested form is transient in Nature, whose resolve is true, enjoys in blissful detachment from all actions triggered by expectations. This enjoyer is *Brahman*" (Chhandogya Upanishad III-14-2).

Expectations are the result of the interplay of the awareness that is one's individual Self and the three virtues (*Gunas*)— goodness (*Sattva*), passion (*Rajas*) and chaos (*Tamas*) that constitutes the mind of the manifested being. Goodness or *Sattvic guna* leads to clarity in understanding Nature's working and alignment of expectations with reality. *Rajas* and *Tamasic gunas* lead to varying degrees of divergence from the real or true (*Sat*) understanding thereby causing unfulfilled expectations.

6.3 Tightrope of expectations

From Singular blissful joy of pure awareness arises the bursting for expression, an irrepressible urge through *Manomaya* (The power of the mind – Mano - by which the universe becomes manifest; the illusion or appearance of the phenomenal world) leading to the rise of embodied beings in Nature bound by the laws of *Karma* (action and reaction).

It is through *Manomaya* that actions arise from the manifested being leading to reactions and effects in accordance with Nature's laws of cause and effect, action and reaction. Each such play of actions and consequent reactions is indeed fructified in Nature's realm of space as a manifestation that adds to myriad plurality. Such a manifestation journeys through Nature's essence of time and transience from origin through growth, plateau, decline and eventual demise of such manifested beings over time. Thereby adding to the awe-inspiring display of Nature for each being's expectations to manifest itself and enjoy that of other manifestations. It is the tightrope of expectations that each manifestation in Nature shares with every other manifestation. Each manifestation originates from and dissolves into the singular sentience of Self that connects and binds each one of us, every manifested being!

Understanding, acceptance and realization of the origins, existence and demise of one's own manifestation is an important aspect of one's path of transcendence to being one with Self.

"Self can be defined as that from which proceed the origin, sustenance and dissolution of this universe" (Sutra 2 – *Janmadyasya yatah*).

7. Connected co-existence of Self
(Brahman)

"The secrets of evolution, are time and death.
There's an unbroken thread that stretches from
those first cells to us."
— Carl Sagan, Cosmos

Each individual Self (*Atman*) within every manifested being is connected to every 'other' individual Self (*Brahman*). Each individual Self itself being connected to the universal Self (*Brahman*) by being in essence the same as the non-transient, singular sentient awareness that is Self (*Brahman*). This is connected co-existence.

Further, the individual manifested being is engulfed by and connected to the transience, plurality and insentience in Nature. Nature's essence of transient insentient plurality is a force that is external to every manifested being and drives it throughout its existence in Nature.

Each manifested being in turn is connected to the individual Self (*Brahman*) which silently witnesses and enjoys in blissful detachment, the transient insentient plurality of Nature through the manifested being.

The *Sat* refers to the universal Self (*Brahman*), the singular reality (truth); the *Jiva* as its manifested being. By the term *Jiva* we must understand the individual manifestation of the awareness that is *Brahman* which anchors the body and supports the breath of life (*Prana*) in the Jiva.

Individual Self or *Atman* is understood to be the same as the universal Self (*Brahman*) which co-exists with the manifested being. The *Atman* is the individualized pervasiveness of universal Self in all manifested beings.

Awareness of the co-existence and connectedness between Self (*Brahman*) on the one hand and transience of Nature on the other is the key to discovering individual Self and eventually the universal Self (*Brahman*). Awareness can be achieved whence focusing on cognizing the individual Self through one's *Sattvic guna* or goodness, whilst simultaneously being aware of the forces of one's own *Rajasic* (passion) and *Tamasic* (chaos) *gunas* playing in Nature's transience, plurality and insentience. Being one with Self provides the awareness that allows each force to play out while anchored in Self.

Transcendence to universal Self or emancipation from transience is declared in the scriptures to be for "one who is devoted to Self, who is completely immersed in it; who is one with it"(Chandogya Upanishad VI-14-2).

The following sections elaborate on the essence of *Brahman* (Self).

7.1 Bliss of *Brahman* (Self)

Nature, by its very essence is transient insentient plurality, thereby diffusing and draining sometimes, converging and making one grow at other times. Its very essence is ebb and flow. In contrast to Nature is the individual Self within each one of us.

With the discovery of and engagement with one's individual Self within, comes a sense of boldness, fearlessness and enjoyment while engaging with one's external world that is one of transience, plurality and insentience. That sense of un-fearing, unfettered enjoyment is bliss – the essence of one's individual Self; and indeed universal Self.

Fleeting though it undoubtedly will be in one's early stages of evolution in discovering and reflecting on *Brahman*, one's sustained closeness and eventual realization of one's individual Self through oneness with it and eventual transcendence to the universal Self leads to "a state of pure eternal blissful awareness which is the *Brahman*" (Taittiriya Upanishad. III-6-1, 5.2 and Brihadaranyaka Upanishad III-9-27 which outline a doctrine that identifies and describes this real Self).

The state of transcendence when engaging with the transience surrounding us without fear and unfettered bliss is born out of the discovery and realization that the essence of Nature i.e. its transience is non-sustaining, impermanent and unreal.

As one progresses on the path of increased focus on discovering, reflecting realizing and transcending to Self, one rests in that which is invisible, bodiless, indefinable, fearless i.e. one's individual Self (*Brahman*). Such is the state of true transcendence, emancipation, enlightenment, liberation and release (*Moksha*) that lies beyond the manifested world with its cyclical change (*Samsara*).

7.1.1   Universal bliss

Universal bliss is when the individual Self rests in the knowledge of and eventual oneness with the universal Self (*Brahman*), the source of bliss. *Sruti* 14 declares that universal *Brahman* is the single source of bliss (*Taddhetu vyapadesaccha*). Professing therein that the source of all bliss and indeed the source of bliss in the individual Self is the universal Self.

"It is *Brahman* who is the source of bliss for all *(Esha hyevanandayati)*.

"For it alone causes bliss" – (Taittiriya UpanishadII-7).

7.2 Non-manifested Imperishability of Self

Being beyond time and space implies being non-embodied i.e. non-manifested, all pervasive i.e. being both without and within every being, origin-less and perennial (imperishable), being "without attachment to the rhythm (transience) of breath and mind"(Mundaka Upanishad II-1-2).

"The non-manifestation *(Avyaktam)* and non-differentiation *(Avyakrita)* of the universal Self makes Self the imperishable potentiality or the seed of all possible names and forms, containing the subtle parts of the material elements" (Purusha of Chhandogya Upanishad - chapters 1, 6 and 7 and Kaundlaya Upanishad I-3-15). Self is a state that is in itself not an effect of anything and a source of all effects.

"The realized being within i.e. the individual Self is *Tat tvam asi* (that who already is *Brahman*) " (Mundaka Upanishad II-1-10).

The individual Self is that which feeds or holds back, encourages or discourages, directs those components of the manifested being (thoughts, feelings and actions) to which it itself is connected; eventually handing control over to them in its manifested existence. Allowing it to take a course dictated to it by the manifested being's own expectations, thoughts and actions that drive it to walk the tightrope of expectations.

While itself being the silent witness, the individual non-manifested Self is the harbinger of infinite potentialities and possibilities.

"The higher knowledge is this by which the indestructible is known or realized. That which cannot be seen nor seized, which is without origin and qualities, without hands and feet, the eternal, all-pervading, omnipresent, infinitesimal, that which is imperishable, that it is which the wise consider as the source of all beings"(Mundaka Upanishad I-1-5 and 6).

Recognizing the binds of transience and plurality viz. limitations of space and time enables one to extricate oneself from such binds. Fleetingly initially and gradually progressing to increased persistence in the timeless and space-less universe of Self. Subsequently progressing from connectedness to an established state of oneness with Self.

7.3 Pervasiveness of Self *(Brahman)*

Myriad manifestations of transience and plurality that one experiences during one's manifested being's existence in Nature (anchored by and connected to one's individual Self) provides a good starting point to understand the pervasiveness of Self (*Brahman*) that co-exists with Nature's transience, plurality and insentience.

Nature abounds and revels in its transience and plurality that is sustained across time and space by striking its own balance. Its cyclicality (of varying forms in constantly changing shapes and sizes) is essentially based on balance between its laws of creation, sustenance and destruction of individual beings while successfully sustaining itself and its laws.

Self in turn is omnipresent in Nature's laws and its manifested beings. Enabling Nature to sustain itself across time and space. Nature's own Self co-exists with Nature's plurality and transience. It is a tenuously balanced co-existence of transience, plurality and insentience on the one hand and the non-transient, singular, sentient awareness that is Self on the other.

7.3.1   Discovering pervasive awareness

Recognizing that every manifested being in Nature is nothing but another manifestation of one's own manifested self lies at the heart of understanding the pervasiveness of the aware non-manifested beings, the individual Selves. The individual Selves co-exist in the multitude of manifested beings as a part of an ascending cascade of Self through to one universal Self (*Brahman*).

This pervasiveness is discussed in the scriptures as: "The Sun does not shine by itself; nor do the moon and the stars, nor the lightning, much less the fire. When it (*Brahman*) shines, everything shines"(Mundaka Upanishad II-2-10 and Kathopanisad II-ii-15).

7.4 Discovering Brahman in Nature

Seeing transience for what it is – non-persistent and unreal – is the starting point for one's moving away from it, one's transcendence to the reality of *Brahman*, the awareness that is Self. Such a discovery of Nature's essence of transient insentient plurality can be a strong motivator for the ardent individual Self that is aware of the restlessness within the manifested being. Anchoring one's being to the shifting sands of transience and plurality - an unreal state of *Maya* (The power by which the universe becomes manifest; the illusion or appearance of the phenomenal world) takes one into the oblivion of isolation.

Conversely, realizing the reality of Self provides a reality of oneness with a non-changing, singular reality. It leads to discovering that the only reality, the only truth to invest one's being in is *Brahman*. It signals the start of one's move from transience to Self. A discovery which eventually leads to transcendence towards a state of connectedness, a oneness of being that in essence each being already is – *Tat Twam Asi*.

7.4.1   Steps to discovering Brahman in Nature

Discovering how to step out of plurality – name, form and individual identity – to a common singular reality that connects beings, albeit still in the realm of plurality serves as a good starting point. Such a reality is one's breath – *Prana* (universal life-giving force), which is a singular reality that connects every manifested being. The meditation on *Prana*, one's own breath, exposes one to the rhythm, the transience in Nature. It helps in transcending beyond the individual embodiment with attributes (like name, form etc.) to a connectedness that binds all living beings, the rhythm of breath.

"Transcendence begins with one's 'name' and goes higher and higher, step by step, till ultimately reaching the highest truth which is the universal Self, *Bhuma* (*Brahman*) or the Infinite" (Seventh chapter of the Chhandogya Upanishad).

Transcendence is "a state where one sees nothing else, hears nothing else, understands nothing else, that is the universal intransient, sentient singularity that is *Brahman"* (Chhandogya Upanishad VIII-22-24).

7.4.2 Ephemerality of one's existence in Nature

One's identity and attachments are a natural corollary of one's manifested existence in Nature. It is a necessity that ensures conformity of one's manifestation to the laws of Nature bound by time and space.

Definition is the hallmark of identity. It is a definition in terms of all that is in the realm of Nature – shape, size, location, color, one's features etc. The list goes on. There is then the definition that is created within one's manifested being – one's thoughts and feelings; one's own perception of one's own identity.

Further, there is the definition born out of one's actions. That by which the innumerable 'other' plural beings sense you, think and are aware of you. It is indeed how one internally is aware of and thinks of one's manifested being.

There are then one's feelings of attachment to that which lies both within and outside one's self. These are one's attachments to one's physical necessities that sustain one's manifestation in Nature - attachments to sustenance and procreation, attachments to other beings – one's parents, siblings, offspring, friends, community etc. Indeed, an attachment to try ensuring persistence ad infinitum of one's manifested being. Such attachments, one discovers, are subject to Nature's laws of origin, growth, plateau, decline and demise; like everything in Nature's realm. Transience and plurality are in essence ephemeral.

Discovery of one's own awareness of attachments being ephemeral is the start of one's transcendence, one's liberation from plurality and achieving oneness with Self!

7.4.3 Brahman beyond Ephemerality

In Nature's infinite states of being, there is embedded a state of non-transience, non-plurality in itself. Not being an effect of any cause. This is Self (*Brahman*) in the midst of Natures' plurality and transience.

Conception of such a state of pure being, of Self, lies beyond all sensory aids that enable the grasping and understanding of Nature and its laws.

In the midst of Nature, discovering the individual Self (*Brahman*) within every being is the realm sought out in the yearning; as an adequate response to Nature and its transience. Such a Self is ensconced in every being's core, offering itself to be reflected on. This is the same essence universally pervading all of Nature and its embodied beings – "The universal Self (*Vaisvanara, Brahman*), permeating across the entire universe and is identical in essence to one's individual Self" (Chhandogya Upanishad V.18.1-2).

Focusing on and discovering the individual Self within oneself leads to an awareness of completeness within oneself. It is an awareness of wholeness that does not need nor desire anything else. It does not even need nor desire the awareness of wholeness or completeness! It is an awareness that does not call for any action. For action is required only when something is expected. It is an awareness that does not need to be resisted nor accepted. It is an awareness that just is. It is an awareness that which is already whole, complete - *Tat tvam asi* (that which one already is).

Beyond one's individual Self is the absolute universal Self *(Para Brahman)*. It is the basis or resting place of all that is. It is all there is. "It is which the heaven, the earth, and the sky are woven into, as also the mind with all the senses. Know Him alone as the Brahman. That is the bridge of immortality" (Mundaka Upanishad II-2-5).

8. Moving from Transience to Self (*Brahman*)

"Gradual liberation or emancipation (*Krama Mukti*) from Nature's transience can be achieved in degrees only by meditating on the non-manifested being (*Brahman*)" (Prasna Upanishad V-5)

The reality of Self (*Brahman*) is non-manifested out of necessity. Non-transient, singular, sentient Self (*Brahman*) is the only reality that offers a platform to witness and enjoy the transience and plurality of Nature. It is a transience to be transcended from for the yearner who has experienced it to the fullest and is ready to grow out of it into the reality of Self.

The reality of Self is essentially everything that Nature with its transience, plurality and insentience is not. Nature provides unique manifestations of shape, size, color etc. that is in a constant state of transience and plurality (i.e. countless uniquely manifested beings due to Nature's plurality). The non-transient, singular awareness that *Brahman* offers is non-manifested.

Further, the platform of non-transient, aware and sentient singularity that is the Self is the only reality that enables witnessing, enjoying actions and desired outcomes out of infinite potentialities in Nature's realm of space and time.

8.1 Meditation and transcendence

By implication, the one who yearns cannot aspire to transcend by being beholden to manifested objects and beings. While such manifested or material beholden-ness could assist in focusing one's mind (primarily because it is the only familiar environment that manifested beings find themselves in), it cannot and does not assist in realizing and transcending to oneness with Self. In fact it prevents such transcendence.

"The Highest *Brahman* (Self) is described as being realizable through meditation as an object by vision (*Ikshana*)"(Prasna Upanishad V-2).

Misjudged "focus and reflection on manifestations and their source (Hiranyagarbha – source of creation of the manifested cosmos) as a means to transcend is considered as lacking an understanding of the reality of *Brahman* from the transcendental perspective. It is within the realm of illusion, *Maya* (The power by which the universe becomes manifest; the illusion or appearance of the phenomenal world)" (Prasna Upanishad V-5).

8.1.1 Discovering non-manifested reality and sentience

The existence of one's manifested Self in plurality is a harnessed experience; born out of the desire to witness and experience plurality that is shared with all other manifested beings.

Such an existence allows free rein to all manifested selves to be themselves in their transience through plurality. One's existence in Nature is bound by the laws of Nature; laws that bind and separate, merge and demerge, maintaining the subtle balance that provides the awe-inspiring transient spectacle for each manifested being to immerse in and enjoy. Such laws maintain a balance which in itself is *Brahman*'s awareness!

Sentient awareness is the marker of any manifested being's degree of transcendence. The zenith of transcendence being an awareness that allows for the eventuating of oneness with the universal Self. It is a state of being that allows oneness with the universal Self away from the constrained plurality of Nature.

Such awareness is the essence of non-manifested reality offered by Self; which one already is (*Tat Twam Asi*).

8.2 Plurality's connectedness to Self

Reflecting on our senses of touch, sight, sound, smell and taste (which are one's tools to partake of what Nature's plurality has to offer) provides a good starting point to assist in one's understanding of how plurality is linked to the individual Self within oneself. The senses are essentially the connectedness of one's body to the world around – a world constituted of objects (born out of the plurality in Nature); objects that can be touched, seen, heard, smelt and tasted. Such sensing enables one to characterize and discriminate each object in relation to oneself and form judgments about. All aimed at enabling survival of one's manifested being in Nature's plurality.

Characterization and discrimination are enabled by one's mind, armed with intellect. One's mind is the one that holds facts of one's experiences while co-existing and interacting with objects and beings other than oneself. It also drives one's actions (performed by bodily parts like one's arms, legs etc.) as part of the process of interaction. It holds the outcomes (or reactions) of such actions thereby assisting in understanding the principles of cause and effect that are fundamental in Nature. Mind and intellect not only hold experiences and outcomes (in one's memory), it also holds knowledge for future reference and use.

The awareness that is one's individual Self is the centerpiece of one's manifested being's existence in Nature. Sensing, knowing and learning are aimed at ensuring the continued witnessing, experiencing and enjoyment for the individual Self within.

Each such manifested being resides in Nature's realm of space. The individual Self within each manifested being enables experiencing the space around - air, water, fire, land etc.

Beyond the manifested beings and objects, are the non-manifested potentialities that reside in each such being. Such potentialities feed into Nature's laws that play out probabilities, possibilities and potentialities and manifest as actions and reactions in Nature's realm of space and time.

8.2.1   Potentialities of non-manifested, pervasive *Brahman*

The non-manifested aspect of *Brahman* (Self) and the Nature's laws that provide the framework for such non-manifested potentialities as manifested actions and reactions is where and whence co-existence, the linking of Self *(Brahman)* to plurality resides.

"There is one *Aja* (Creative power of *Brahman*'s inherent energy) producing manifold offspring of the same Nature" (Svetasvatara Upanishad IV-5). It is the Self that stirs out manifested entities from 'no thing' – the essence of Self's co-existence with Nature.

Self's essence of pure awareness in Nature's stage of plurality, transience, cause and effect, action and reaction is unique in a universe constituted of myriad forms in constant change from creation through demise.

Self's uniqueness also lies in its universality i.e. omnipresence in every manifested being in all of Nature's dimensions. Regardless of shape and form, regardless of state of transience of any being in Nature – animate or inanimate, Self's awareness pervades the plurality and transience of every manifested being in Nature. **It is not plurality that is unique but Self!**.

It is this unique aware Self that connects every manifested form through its co-existence in every manifested being. It is this unique Self in the midst of myriad transience and plurality that experiences everything that plays out in Nature; while being the one that connects and anchors every being. It is a singular Self (*Brahman*) that is an anchor and enjoyer of plurality and transience.

8.3 Connectedness to universal Self

While the individual Self in every manifested being (*Atman*) is connected to the universal Self (*Brahman*) by their mutual non-transience and singular sentient awareness, it is also quite different from universal *Brahman* or the Supreme Self in that the individual Self is bound in the manifested being by limiting adjuncts (*Upadhis*) due to ignorance (*Avidya*). The difference is illusory or unreal from the absolute or transcendental view point in that it is due to the individual Self's 'attachment' to the manifested being that causes the difference. This difference disappears when the illusion of attachment disappears and the individual Self realizes through knowledge of the Self (*Brahmajnana*) its true essence i.e. the oneness with universal Self (*Brahman*). "When the Self is known all this is known, all this is that Self" (Sutra 126).

8.4 Co-existence of Nature and Self

Co-existence of Self and Nature's plurality and transience is an essential element of manifestation wherein any manifestation (transient and plural, bound by cause and effect, time and space) has as its ally the Self, the anchor to view and experience plurality for what it is – transient and unreal when perceived from the perspective of its own individual Self and indeed the universal Self within the ocean of plurality (i.e. numerous 'other' beings).

Self is wherein transience is seen to be what it is in the context of the reality of Self (*Brahman*); which is pure non-transient singular sentience. Plurality has to be seen for what it is in the context of the singularity of Self as "mere thought forms created by non-transience and non-plurality of Self"[8.2]. Thought forms in turn are 'subjective' (i.e. originating in each manifested being), conditioned (learnt) and coordinated (across numerous beings) at times, random and individualistic at others.

What is 'real' in the ocean of plurality and transience for an individual manifested being is the 'connectedness through non-transient singular sentient awareness' to each being.

Consequently, every manifested being in Nature can be viewed as "*Brahman*, by its power of multiplying itself in many thousand (plural) forms and in them walking about on earth. In some it may enjoy the objects, in others it may undergo dire penance, and finally again withdraw them all, just as the sun withdraws its many rays."[8.3]

"Inherent in such co-existence is the sentience in the individual Selves merging into universal sentient *Brahman* in a state of latency. This latency, when manifested, is transient insentient plurality manifesting itself out from Brahman; essentially as a transient pluralistic reflection of *Brahman*."[8.3.]

8.5 Discovering Brahman through detachment

The impermanence of every manifestation in Nature's plurality rises and dissolves. When plurality dissolves, there is only singular Self. Occurrence of such dissolution is ongoing in Nature. Beings come to be and dissolve all the time.

Demise of anything or any being that exists in Nature is the means of being dissolved. The pervasive plurality in Nature is re-absorbed in Self; from whence it arose in the first place. *Brahman* alone is where the entirety of plurality plays out and is eventually consumed.

One's individual Self, on the other hand, is essentially immutable; unlike the rest of one's manifestation which is bound by Nature's essentials of time and space – transience and plurality, origin and demise.

Immutability of the individual Self (the *Brahman* within) is due to its essence of being untouched by space and time. Transience, singularity and sentience, are the essence of Self. It is detached from the plurality of one's manifestation in Nature.

Discovering that detachment can only come from realizing the real essence of one's manifested being – a transient impermanence originating from Self, playing itself out in the backdrop of detached Self and dissolving back into Self.

Brahman alone being where the entirety of plurality (including one's individual manifested being) plays out and is eventually consumed.

8.6 Discovering oneness with Self

Recognizing Nature's essence of transience, plurality, and insentience provides the foundation for one to discover one's true position in Nature's ever-shifting sands. It also leads to understanding the existence of one's restlessness and yearning. It is a restlessness and yearning to seek out and understand the essence of one's own individual existence in Nature. It persists till one discovers one's individual Self *(Brahman)*. For it is that individual Self which is aware of the restlessness in the first place.

It is a discovery which sets one on the path to reflect on the essence of such an individual Self. Which when followed with unwavering focus leads to a state of being which lies beyond mere understanding – a state of realization (being one with one's true Self) which is transcendence into oneness with the individual Self and eventually the universal Self.

Beyond oneness with one's individual Self is the realm of the universal Self. Which when understood and realized, leads to transcendence to being one with that which is one's true essence, that which one already is - *Tat Tvam Asi*.

The challenge in discovering Self is recognizing its non-manifestation. Which is its very essence. Self *(Brahman)* is everything that Nature is not viz. transient, plural, insentient manifestations in space and time.

Discovering, reflecting on, realizing and transcendence to the reality of Self demands capabilities beyond sensory and intellectual reasoning.

It requires skills that develop from deep reflection on the reality of Self (*Brahman*) that is non-transient, singular sentience.

Once discovered, the path of reflection for the individual being begins. Deep reflection on the non-manifested could lead eventually to realization of and transcendence to or oneness with *Brahman*. Understanding Self (*Brahman*) cannot be objectified. There is, in essence, no differentiation between the object being understood, the Self and the one that is the subject of understanding (one's individual Self). In Self, there is no 'other'. There is only 'one' Self - *Tat tvam asi*.

"Having discovered *Brahman* in oneself, a wise being, by means of deep reflection on Brahman within, which in spite of being unseen, leaves joy and sorrow (of transience) far behind. Thereby transcending to oneness with *Brahman*." (Kathopunishad I-3-9).

Reference

0.1   https://en.wikipedia.org

For definition of philosophical terms used in the Brahma Sutras

0.2   https://www.merriam-webster.com/dictionary

For translation of Sanskrit words into English

0.3   https://theosophy.wiki/en

For definition of philosophical terms used in the Brahma Sutras

0.4   https://www.yogapedia.com

For definition of philosophical terms used in the Brahma Sutras

1.1   Section I.1.1 (1) of "Brahma Sutras - Text, word-to-word meaning, translation and commentary by Sri Swami Sivananda" (Published by The Divine Life Society, P.O. P.O. Shivanandanagar – 249 192, Tehri-Garhwal, Uttarakhand, Himalayas, India – 2008)

3.1   The Four Means
1.) Viveka - discrimination. This is the intellectual ability to discriminate, or discern, between the real and the unreal. Vedanta defines the real as being permanent and the unreal as being temporary. The absolutely real, *Brahman*, is eternal. It lasts forever.
2.) Vairagya - dispassion, detachment.

There is a logical order in the four means. After sufficient practice of viveka, the temporary, ephemeral nature of the world and its objects becomes obvious and a natural lack of attraction to them takes place. This is vairagya. One should then endeavor to become more dispassionate in order to purify the mind and improve one's concentration and steadiness of mind.

3.) Shad-sampat - means the six virtues. This practice actually consists in developing six qualities or virtues. They are:

>Sama – Tranquility or control of mind. Calmness. This is the ability to keep the mind within and unaffected by the external world.
>Dama – Control of the senses. This consists in not letting the senses run out towards the sense objects. To the question, "Why do we need to control the senses when we can directly work on sama and control the mind itself – the mind being superior and more powerful than the senses?", the vedantins answer: If one were able to control the mind perfectly, dama would be unnecessary, otherwise it is a more powerful strategy to work on the mind apparatus from all sides.
>Uparati – Renunciation of activities which are not duties. Following the last two practices, the mind is so peaceful and calm most desires have been eradicated and there is no more reason to perform the activities in which most people indulge.
>Titiksha – Endurance, forbearance of the pairs of opposites. The mind must become strong enough to not waver in the face of the opposites: success and failure, hot and cold, pleasure and pain, sunshine and rain, etc.

Shraddha – Faith. It is defined by Sri Sankaracharya as faith in one's guru, god, the self (atman) and the scriptures (shastras).

Samadhana – Perfect concentration, one-pointedness of the mind. It takes a great degree of mastery to reach this level. Few reach it.

4.) Mumukshutva

Mumukshutva means intense longing for liberation. When this stage is reached, moksha (liberation) is not one of the jnani's desires, it is not even the biggest desire, it is the only desire.

Reference: http://shaktianandayoga.com/teachings/four-paths/jnana-yoga/the-four-means-to-salvation/

© 2020 - Shaktiananda Yoga

4.1 *Tat tvam asi* - a Sanskrit phrase, translated variously as "Thou art that," (That thou art, That art thou, You are that, or That you are, or You're it). It is one of the Mahāvākyas (Grand Pronouncements) that originally occurs in originally occurs in the Chandogya Upanishad 6.8.7

4.2 *Moksha*, also called *vimoksha, vimukti* and *mukti*, is a term in Hinduism, Buddhism, Jainism and Sikhism which refers to various forms of emancipation, enlightenment, liberation, and release

Source: Wikipedia:
https://en.wikipedia.org/wiki/Moksha

8.3 Quote from section I.3.26 (93) of "Brahma Sutras - Text, word-to-word meaning, translation and commentary by Sri Swami Sivananda" (Published by THE DIVINE LIFE SOCIETY, P.O.

SHIVANANDANAGAR—249 192, Tehri-Garhwal, Uttarakhand, Himalayas, India – 2008)

7.1 Quote from section I.2.17 (53) of "Brahma Sutras - Text, word-to-word meaning, translation and commentary by Sri Swami Sivananda" (Published by THE DIVINE LIFE SOCIETY, P.O. SHIVANANDANAGAR—249 192, Tehri-Garhwal, Uttarakhand, Himalayas, India – 2008)

7.2 Quote from section I.2.24 (85) of "Brahma Sutras - Text, word-to-word meaning, translation and commentary by Sri Swami Sivananda" (Published by THE DIVINE LIFE SOCIETY, P.O. SHIVANANDANAGAR—249 192, Tehri-Garhwal, Uttarakhand, Himalayas, India – 2008)

8.1 The seventh chapter of the Chhandogya Upanishad (where Sanatkumara gives instructions to Narada).
As quoted in "Brahma Sutras - Text, word-to-word meaning, translation and commentary by Sri Swami Sivananda" (Published by The Divine Life Society, P.O. Shivanandnagar—249 192, Tehri-Garhwal, Uttarakhand, Himalayas, India – 2008)

23.3 Quote from section I.3.26 (93) of "Brahma Sutras - Text, word-to-word meaning, translation and commentary by Sri Swami Sivananda" (Published by THE DIVINE LIFE SOCIETY, P.O. SHIVANANDANAGAR—249 192, Tehri-Garhwal, Uttarakhand, Himalayas, India – 2008)

Appendix 1 - Brahma Sutras chapter 1 main headings (Adhikaranams)

Following are the list of *Adhikaranams* (topics) and Sutras (aphorisms) of Brahma Sutras Chapter 1 as contained in each Section of this book

Book section 1-Discovering restlessness and yearning
Topic 1 (Sutra 1)–*Jijnasadhikaranam* - The enquiry into *Brahman* and its pre-requisites

Book section 2-The experiential world and reality beyond
Topic 2 (Sutra 2)–*Janmadyadhikaranam* - Definition of *Brahman*

Book section 3-Discovering Self (*Brahman*)
Topic 3 (Sutra 3)–*Sastrayonitvadhikaranam* - *Brahman* is realizable only through the scriptures

Book section 4-Brahma Sutras and Self
Topic 4 (Sutra 4)- *Samanvayadhikaranam* - *Brahman* the main purport of all Vedantic texts

Book section 5-Individual Self (*Atman*)
Topic 14 (Sutras 42-43)- *Guhapravishtadhikaranam*
The dwellers in the heart of a manifested being are the individual Self (*Atman*) and *Brahman*
Topic 15 (Sutras 44-48)- *Antaradhikaranam*: The anchor within the eye (as an example of any manifested being) is *Brahman*
Topic 16 (Sutras 49-51)- *Antaryamyadhikaranam*: The internal (to the manifested being) anchor is *Brahman*

Topic 23 (Sutras 77-84)- *Daharadhikaranam*: The *Dahara* or the Small *Akasa* (i.e. the ether) is *Brahman*

Book section 6- *Manomaya*
Topic 5 (Sutras 5-11)- *Ikshatyadyadhikaranam: Brahman* as universal awareness *principle* is the single universal source
Topic 12 (Sutras 32-39)- *Sarvatra Prasiddhyadhikaranam*: The *Manomaya* is *Brahman*
Topic 22 (Sutra 76)- *Ikshatikarmavyapadesadhikaranam*: The object of meditation is to be *Brahman*
Topic 35 (Sutra 120-121)- *Karanatvadhikaranam: Brahman* is the single source
Topic 38 (Sutra 129-133)- *Prakrityadhikaranam: Brahman* is both the efficient and the material cause
Daharadhikaranam: The *Dahara* or the Small *Akasa* (i.e. the ether) is *Brahman*

Book section 7- Universal Self (*Brahman*)
Topic 6 (Sutras 12-31)- *Anandamayadhikaranam*: *Anandamaya* (universally pervasive pure bliss) is *Para Brahman* (supreme Brahman)
Topic 7 (Sutras 20-21)- *Antaradhikaranam:* That which is the innermost Self of light and enables sight (the Sun and the eye) is *Brahman*.
Topic 8 (Sutra 22)- *Akasadhikaranam:*
The word *Akasa* (ether) must be understood as *Brahman*.
Topic 9 (Sutra 23)- *Pranadhikaranam*: The word *Prana* (breath) must be understood as *Brahman*
Topic 10 (Sutras 24-27)- *Jyotischaranadhikaranam*: The light is *Brahman*
Topic 11 (Sutras 28-31)- *Pratardanadhikaranam*: *Prana* is *Brahman*
Topic 13 (Sutras 40-41)- *Attradhikaranam:* The final abode for all manifestations is *Brahman*

Topic 17 (Sutras 52-54)- *Adrisyatvadhikaranam*: That which cannot be seen is *Brahman*

Topic 18 (Sutras 55-63)- *Vaisvanaradhikaranam*: *Vaisvanara* (That which symbolizes Nature) is *Brahman*

Topic 19 (Sutras 64-70)- The source and eventual destination of heaven, earth etc. is *Brahman*

Topic 20 (Sutras 71-72)- *Bhumadhikaranam*: *Bhuma* (earth) is *Brahman*

Topic 21 (Sutras 73-75)- *Aksharadhikaranam*: *Akshara* (the indestructible) is *Brahman*

Topic 24 (Sutras 85-86)- *Anukrityadhikaranam*: Everything shines after *Brahman*

Topic 25 (Sutras 87-88)- *Pramitadhikaranam:* The smallest conceivable being (person of the size of a thumb) is *Brahman*

Topic 28 (Sutra 102)- *Kampanadhikaranam*: *Prana* (breath) in which everything trembles is *Brahman*

Topic 29 (Sutra 103)- *Jyotiradhikaranam*: 'Light' is *Brahman*

Topic 30 (Sutra 104)- *Arthantaratvadivyapadesadhikaranam: Akasa* (ether) is *Brahman*

Topic 31 (Sutras 105-106)- *Sushuptyutkrantyadhikaranam*: All knowledge is *Brahman*

Topic 36 (Sutras 122-124)- *Balakyadhikaranam*: The single source (e.g. the maker of the Sun, Moon, etc. is *Brahman* and not *Prana* (breath) nor the individual Self within the individual manifested being

Topic 37 (Sutras 125-128)- *Vakyanvayadhikaranam* The *Atman* (individual Self) to be seen through hearing and meditating upon the Upanishads is *Brahman* and not the manifested being nor the individual Self

Topic 39 (Sutra 134)- *Sarvavyakhyanadhikaranam*:

Sankhya philosophy (which is based on principles of Nature (*Prakriti*) being the source of all manifestations is counter to Vedic philosophy

Appendix 2 - Association of Upanishads with Vedas

The Aitreya and Kaushitaki are the *Mukhya* (main) Upanishads of the Rig Veda (which has a total of ten Upanishads).

The Chhandogya and Kena are the *Mukhya* (main) Upanishads of the Sama Veda (which has a total of sixteen Upanishads).

The Taittiriya, Svetesvatara, Katha, and Maitryani are the *Mukhya* (main) Upanishads of the Krishna Yajur Veda (which has a total of nineteen Upanishads).

The Brihadaranyaka and Isa are the *Mukhya* (main) Upanishads of the Shukla Yajur Veda(which has a total of thirty-one Upanishads)

The Mundaka, Mandukya and Prasna are the *Mukhya* (main) Upanishads of the Atharva Veda(which has a total of ten Upanishads).

The following is the list of Upanishads that are NOT the *Mukhya* (main) Upanishads for each Veda.

RigVeda   Atmabodha, Mudgala
               (constituting the *Samanya* Upanishads)
               Nirvana
               (constituting the *Sanyasa* Upanishads)
               Tripura, Saubhagya-Laxmi, Bahvrca
               (constituting the *Sakta* Upanishads)
               Aksamalika

(constituting the *Saiva* Upanishads)
Nadabindu
(constituting the *Nadabindu* Upanishads)

SamaVeda Vajrasuchi, Maha, Savitri
(constituting the *Samanya* Upanishads)
Aruni, Maitreya, Brhat-Sannyasa, Kundika (Laghu-Sannyasa)
(constituting the *Sanyasa* Upanishads)
Vasudeva, Avyakta
(constituting the *Vaisnava* Upanishads)
Rudraksha, Jabali
(constituting the *Saiva* Upanishads)
Yogachudamani, Darsana
(constituting the *Yoga* Upanishads)

Krishna YajurVeda

Sarvasara, Sukarahasya, Skanda, Garbha, Sariraka, Ekaksara, ASksi
(constituting the *Samanya* Upanishads)
Brahma, (Laghu, Brihad) Avadhuta, Kathasruti
(constituting the *Sanyasa* Upanishads)
Sarasvati Rahasysa
(constituting the *Sakta* Upanishads)
Narayana, Kali-Santarna
(constituting the *Vaisnava* Upanishads)
Kavalya, Kalagnirudra, Dakshinamurti, Rudrahrdya, Pancabrahma
(constituting the *Saiva* Upanishads)
Amrtabindu, Tejobindu, Amrtanada, Ksurika, Dhyanabindu, Brahmavidya, Yogatattva, Yogasikha, Yogakundalini, Varaha
(constituting the *Yoga* Upanishads)

Shukla YajurVeda

Subala, Mantrika, Niralamba, Paingala, Adhyatma, Muktika
(constituting the *Samanya* Upanishads)
Jabala, Parahamsa, Bhiksuka, Turiyatitavadhuta, Yagnavalkya, Satyayaniya
(constituting the *Sanyasa* Upanishads)
Tarasarara
(constituting the *Vaisnava* Upanishads)
Advaitaraka, Hamsa, Trisikhi, MandalaBrahmana
(constituting the *Yoga* Upanishads)

AtharvaVeda

Atma, Surya, Pranagnihotra
(constituting the *Samanya* Upanishads)
Asrama, Narada-parivrijaka, Parahamsa-parivrijaka, Parabrahma
(constituting the *Sanyasa* Upanishads)
Sita, Devi, Tripuratapani, Bhavana
(constituting the *Sakta* Upanishads)
Nrsimhatapani, Mahanarayana (Tripad vibhuti), Ramarahasya, Ramatapani, Gopalatapani, Krsna, Hayagirva, Dattatreya, Garuda
(constituting the *Vaisnava* Upanishads)
Atharvasiras, Atharvasikha, Brhajjabala, Sarabha, Bhasma, Ganapati
(constituting the *Saiva* Upanishads)
Sandilya, Pasupata, Mahavakya
(constituting the *Yoga* Upanishads)

Appendix 3 – Upanishad Quotes

Quotes relating to Section 2: The experiential world and reality beyond

Following quotes from various Upanishads that so highlight Self *(Brahman)* as the origin of all that exists assist in discovering the essence of Self *(Brahman)* – **Section 2**.

"Being only was in the beginning, one only without a second. It thought 'May I be many, may I grow forth.' It projected fire." (Chhandogya Upanishad VI-2).

"The *Atman* (Self) willed: 'Let me project worlds'. So it projected these worlds" (Aitareya Upanishad I-1-1.2).

"There cannot be any thinking or willing in insentient *Pradhana* (creative power of Nature). It is possible only if the source is an aware and sentient being like *Brahman*". (Commentary in Sutra 5 Reference 0.1).

"All this universe is in essence That (Self); That singular awareness is the Truth. That is *Atman* (Soul). That thou art" (Chhandogya Upanishad VI-8-7).

"That from whence beings are born, that by which, when born they live, that into which they enter at their death, try to know that. That is *Brahman*." (Taittiriya Upanishad III-i).

Following quotes from various Upanishads that so highlight contents of Section 4
"As from a burning fire sparks proceed in all directions, thus from that 'Self' the Pranas

70

proceed each towards its place, from the Pranas the gods, from the gods the worlds" (Kaushitaki Upanishad III-3).

"From that *Brahman* (Self) sprang ether (*Akasa*)" (Taittiriya Upanishad II-1).

Following quotes from various Upanishads that so highlight contents of Section 6

"It reflected, he manifested as Prana" (Prashna Upanishad VI.3 and 4).

"As by one lump of clay all that is made of clay is known, the modification i.e., the effect being a name which merely has its origin in speech, while the truth is that it is merely clay" (Chandogya Upanishad VI-1-14).

"He wished or thought may I be many, may I grow forth." (Chandogya Upanishad VI-2).

"That from which these things are produced, by which, when produced they live, and into which they enter at their dissolution — try to know that. That is Self." (Taittiriya Upanishad III-1).

Following quotes from various Upanishads that so highlight contents of **Section 7**

"Universal *Brahman* (*Sat*) only was in the beginning". (*Chhandogya Upanishad VI-2*).

"After creating fire, water, earth, *Brahman* thought 'let me now enter into these three as this manifested being (Jiva) and evolve names and forms (effects)' (Chhandogya Upanishad VI-3-2).

"*Brahman*, the awareness that is Self is endless without a shore" (Brihadarnyaka Upanishad II-4-12).

"That which is spoken of as the abode, in that which everything exists, which is woven into - is *Brahman*, the Self".

"All that is, have their root in this *Brahman*, their abode in the *Brahman*, their rest in *Brahman*" (Chhandogya Upanishad VI-8-4).

Become aware of the Self (*Brahman*) alone as your Self, the Self of everything (the connectedness). All else is a product of Nature's transience. It is illusory and unreal.

"From death to death goes he who beholds anything different here" (Katha Upanishad II-4-11).

"*Brahman* enables manifestation of everything else (in Nature) but is not manifested by anything else" (Brihadaranyaka Upanishad IV-4-16);

"The entire world of names and forms (plurality) is dependent on *Brahman* and indeed the source of Nature's effulgence." (Brihadaranyaka Upanishad III-17-9);

"Neither the sun, nor the moon, nor the fire illumines that, having gone into which men do not

72

return, that is my highest seat." (Bhagavad Gita, Chapter XV-6);

"The light which abiding in the sun illumines the whole world and that which is in the moon and that which is in the fire, all that light knows *Brahman*" (Bhagavad Gita, Chapter XV-12).

 This reality of Self is one of "All-knowingness (*Sarvajna*) and perception of everything (*Sarvavit*)" (Mundaka Upanishad I-1-9).

Following quotes from various Upanishads that so highlight contents of **Section 8**

"Oneness with *Brahman* (*Kaivalya Moksha*) is arrived at by means of repetition of the syllable OM (A-U-M, *Omkara*). It is that reality of *Brahman* that is in sentient restfulness, free from decay, from death, from fear, the highest" (Prasna Upanishad V-5).
"He attains the end of his journey (oneness with Self), that highest place of any being (symbolized by *Vishnu*)" (Kathopunishad I-3-9).

"By means of reflecting on the Self within leads to realization of its essence - timeless and space less. Which in turn enables one to leave behind the transience of joys and sorrows of one's embodied being" (Kathopunishad I-3-9).